THE ALMSHOUSES OF LONDON

Dulwich College in snow

THE ALMSHOUSES OF LONDON

written and photographed by

CLIVE BERRIDGE

Ashford Press Publishing
Southampton
1987

Published by   Ashford Press Publishing 1987
            1 Church Road
            Shedfield
            Hampshire SO3 2HW

Printed in Great Britain by Hartnolls (1985) Ltd.

Berridge, Clive
    The almshouses of London.
    1. Almshouses — England — London — History
    I. Title
    362.5'83   HV250.L6

ISBN 1-85253-000-6

CONTENTS

COLOUR PLATES

FOREWORD

Those of us who have been nurtured in these Islands enjoy a mighty heritage. Often at times we do not appreciate how rich and colourful our history has been.

In this book Clive Berridge writes in a most attractive way, giving us the benefit of his detailed researching into the voluntary care of people in need in London.

It is deeply moving to read how charitable homes have been voluntarily provided for the shelter of London's poor ever since the 14th century. It appears that the springs of voluntary giving which still flow so freely in our land, have benefited the poor in London throughout past centuries.

I find it exciting to learn of the way in which people, blessed with riches, have felt a social challenge to hold out a helping hand to less fortunate people.

In this generation when the welfare state is supposed to provide for every citizen in the land, it may seem quaint to read of the almshouses that still exist.

However, there are plenty of people who, given the choice, would prefer to have their own little cottage rather than live in an old persons' home, however attractive it may be.

When I was first elected a Member of Parliament the largest building in my constituency was the workhouse. It had hardly changed from the workhouse described by Charles Dickens.

During the past four decades our conscience in this land has been active and we now care for our elderly folk in a much more civilised way.

It is fantastic that Clive Berridge has given so much time to outline for us the heritage of caring that has come down to us. This is a splendid piece of research which will bring a great deal of pleasure to all who love this land.

George Thomas.

Tonypandy.

This book is dedicated to Eddie Carter and to Pauline Bennett, Michelle Ferron, Doreen Procter and Jackie Beckford. Their kindness is reflected in these images.

INTRODUCTION

When Alice Wilkes was walking with her maid servant through mid-16th century rural Islington the plight of the poor of London was probably far from her mind as she noticed a woman milking a cow in a field and decided to try her hand at it. Emerging from behind the cow, a wayward arrow fired by a local archer pierced the high crown of her hat. Shocked but relieved by her narrow escape she declared that, if she ever became a Lady, she would build something on that spot to commemorate her deliverance.

Many years and three husbands later, her maid servant reminded her of that promise and, with money inherited from her late husband Sir Thomas Owen (a Justice of the Court of Common Pleas) the now Dame Alice Owen founded ten almshouses in 1610 for widows from Islington and Clerkenwell together with a school for thirty boys from the same parishes. The building used to stand in St. John Street at the top of Rosebery Avenue and was decorated with arrows on the roof.

A few years later, the famous actor and owner of the Fortune Playhouse Edward Alleyn laid the foundation stone of his 'College of God's Gift' which became known as Dulwich College. It was opened in 1619 and consisted of a warden, a master, almshouses for six poor men and six poor women and a college for the education of twelve boys. In addition Alleyn was responsible for the foundation of three other sets of almshouses for the housing of London's poor in Lamb Alley (Bishopsgate Street), Bath Street (St. Lukes) and at a place called

The Soap-Yard in Southwark. The Soap-Yard almshouses were amalgamated with the Gravel Lane almshouses in October 1862 and eventually relocated at St. Saviours United College in Hamilton Road, West Norwood in 1886 where a number of almshouses and charities were brought together under a scheme of the Charity Commissioners.

The original almshouses of the 'College of God's Gift' still stand on the corner of Gallery Road and College Road in Dulwich – a beautiful cream and white building and one of London's most distinguished almshouses.

In choosing to found almshouses, both Dame Alice and Edward Alleyn were following an example that had been established in England over 500 years before in 1084 when Archbishop Lanfranc founded the Hospital of St. John in Canterbury which is still preserved to this day. As London began to grow, almshouses for the poor slowly began to appear. Among the earliest were Stodies Lane almshouses (1358), and those of John Philpot (1384) and Thomas Knowles (1400) And in his will of 5 September 1421 Sir Richard (Dick) Whittington instructed his executors to found the almshouses in College Hill which became known as Whittington's almshouses. Some of the earlier almshouses were called 'hospitals' or 'colleges' before these terms had acquired their medical and educational connotations and these titles can still be found particularly in south London. Less frequently the term 'asylum' was used.

In Tudor times the building of almshouses was a favourite

form of charitable bequest. Maps of London in the 17th and 18th centuries show the city dotted with them. The parish of Shoreditch alone contained the almshouses of the Haberdashers, Drapers, Weavers, Framework Knitters, Ironmongers and Goldsmiths together with those built as a result of individual bequests. The 19th century saw the founding of many more almshouses both large and small as London grew in size and population and the problems of poverty and bad or non-existent housing became worse. Although they could only scratch the surface of these problems, for the lucky few who found a home in them, the almshouses of London must have seemed like palaces because they provided one of the few alternatives to the horrors of the workhouse or disappearing into the void of London's poverty.

Dame Alice's almshouses have now gone (although the name of her school still appears on a modern building at the top of Rosebery Avenue) as have many of the city's. But others have survived and, although they are one of the least known aspects of London's architecture and history, they provide the city with some of its most beautiful and interesting buildings.

1 NORTH-EAST LONDON

Balthazar Sanchez was born in the Spanish city of Jerez south of Badajoz in Extremadura and was confectioner to Philip of Spain.

He came to England in the royal entourage on the occasion of Philip's marriage to Queen Mary in 1554 and decided to stay. He took the Protestant faith, settled in Tottenham and became (in the words of a contemporary chronicler) 'the first confectioner or comfit maker and grane master of all that professe that trade in this kingdom'. Apart from presumably being responsible for a marked increase in the level of tooth decay amongst the English experiencing the delights of the confectioners art for the first time, in 1596 he founded almshouses in his adopted Tottenham for eight poor single people. They stood in Tottenham High Road and, although Sanchez died in 1602 and was buried in the church of St. Mary Wool-church which was destroyed in the Great Fire of London, the almshouses survived for over 300 years until pulled down in the early 1920s to make way for Burgess's store. But even then his memory was preserved, the building to this day being called 'Sanchez House'.

By contrast, Pound's almshouses (also known as Phesaunt's almshouses) had a rather shorter and unhappier existence. They were built in Tottenham High Road opposite the Wesleyan Chapel. In 1739 Churchwarden Henry Sperling complained about them 'being in a ruinous condition and harbouring several loose, idle and disorderly persons'. Lord Colerane was outraged at the 'horrible abuse' and 'desecration of a church to have nastiness near it'. They were pulled down in 1744 (although later rebuilt). These two neighbouring almshouses illustrate the differing fortunes of the many almshouses which used to exist in north-east London. This area had always been a favourite location for the building of almshouses because of the cheapness of the land and, in previous years before the expansion of London, its peaceful atmosphere. As the East End took shape many of the earlier almshouses were pulled down. But others remained and the area has by far the greatest concentration of surviving almshouses in London. Shoreditch has been the home over the years to some of the great almshouses of the capital but has suffered particularly badly from the growth of London. The first in the parish were those of John Fuller and were built in Old Street where today the Town Hall stands. Of the other almshouses founded by individuals, Allen Badger's almshouses (1698) in Hoxton Street were pulled down in 1873 and Samuel Harwar's (1713) in Kingsland Road demolished in 1879. The great City Livery Companies also built almshouses in the area. The City and East London College occupies the site of what used to be the Worshipful Company of Haberdashers hospital school and almshouses (also known as Robert Aske's almshouses) in Pitfield Street although a plaque on the wall records that the almshouses were taken down in 1873. The Goldsmiths' almshouses were built in 1705 in what is now known as Goldsmith's Row and demolished in 1889 and the same fate

Memorial to a former almshouse. Sanchez House, now Burgess's store, stands on the site of Balthazar Sanchez's almshouses in Tottenham High Road founded in 1596.

befell those of Lady Lumley in Shepherdess Walk, the Hackney Road and Dutch almshouses, the Drapers' in Old Street, Weavers' in Hoxton Street and Framework Knitters' in Kingsland Road although some were to rise again in other districts as we shall see. The last almshouses to be built in Shoreditch were the New Shoreditch almshouses (1852) near St. Mary's Haggerston which were bombed during the Second World War and eventually demolished.

Although these buildings are no longer with us and long forgotten, Shoreditch does still have one of the biggest, finest and best preserved almshouses in London. The Ironmongers' almshouses in Kingsland Road were financed by a bequest from Sir Robert Geffrye (an ironmonger and former Lord Mayor of London) and built in a magnificent style in the early 1700s. The building is one of the greatest surviving examples of Renaissance architecture in Hackney and is built around three sides of a leafy courtyard.

On the façade of the central chapel just above the door is a statue of the founder. A haven of tranquillity amid the bustle of the East End they are the best example of almshouses that have survived by finding new roles for themselves.

In 1908 it appeared that they would go the same way of all the other almshouses in the area when plans were announced to demolish them. But in 1910 they were bought by the London County Council. In 1912 the grounds were opened to the public and in 1914 the building was reopened as the Geffrye Museum.

Today the fourteen almshouses contain a collection of furniture, paintings and household items from previous centuries on display in the old almshouses which have been converted into period rooms. The museum provides a fascinating educational experience for the many children who visit it (both on school trips and in their own free time) and preserves this impressive building in a way that would surely have pleased its founder.

The gateway to the Geffrye Museum (formerly the Ironmongers' almshouses) in Kingsland Road.

The entrance to the Geffrye Museum.

The eastern wing of the Trinity House almshouses.

Staying in the East End of London it is still possible to discover almshouses hidden away despite the many changes in the area in recent years. At the western end of the Mile End Road are the almshouses originally built for the Corporation of Trinity House. Twin plaques on the outside wall record the following:

THIS ALMES HOUSE
wherein 28 decay'd Masters &
Comanders of Ships, or ye widows
of such are maintain'd was built
by ye CORP. of TRINITY HOUSE
AN°. 1695
The ground was given by Capt.
Hen^y. MUDD of Ratcliff and
Elder Brother, whose Widow
did also Contribute

Badly damaged during the Second World War, they were superbly restored and are now used as council housing. Two rows of houses separated by a lawn and an avenue of trees lead up to the building's most eye-catching feature – its former chapel with a clock tower topped by a weather vane. One of the most pleasant scenes in the East End, they were believed by some to be the work of Sir Christopher Wren and were nearly lost in the 1890s when plans were announced to demolish them. A furious outcry including letters to The Times ensued and they were mercifully saved by the Charity Commissioners.

Also in the Mile End Road, the famous old Peoples' Palace was built on the site of Bancroft's almshouses and Lewis Newbery's almshouses (1688) which used to stand in the Mile End Road were removed to a new site at Pellipar Close in Palmers Green in 1891 where they were joined three years later by the almshouses of Sir Andrew Judd which had been founded

The beautiful chapel of the Trinity House almshouses stands proudly framed by a tree.

6

THIS ALMES HOUS
wherein 28 decay'd Masters
Comanders of Ships, or y Widow
of such are maintain'd)was built
by y CORP. of TRINITY HOUS
AN° 1695
The Ground was given by Capt
HENy MUDD of Rattcliff an
Elder Brother, whose Widow
did also Contribute

One of the plaques on the outside wall of the Trinity House almshouses that records the founding of these buildings in 1695.

in 1551 at Great St. Helens in the City of London. The Skinners' almshouses survived here until the mid-1960s when they were partially destroyed by fire. The new ones which stand there today are of a very modern Swedish housing design but plaques and statues brought from the ancient almshouses are on display in the grounds.

Just to the south in Nightingale Road, Wood Green can also be found the new home that was found for several of the Shoreditch almshouses that were demolished. The buildings of the United Charities of St. Leonard include those of Fuller and Harwar from Shoreditch. Back in the East End, Norton Folgate's almshouses stand in Puma Court off the Commercial Road opposite the bustle of Spitalfields market where they were rebuilt in 1860 to replace the original ones of 1728 which were demolished.

Much further along the Commercial Road, Stepney still has one old almshouse building in the shape of George Smith's design for the rebuilt Lady Jane Mico's almshouses for widows which have stood at the corner of Belgrave Street and Stepney High Street since 1856 despite being bombed in March 1941. Lady Mico was the wife of Sir Samuel Mico who was a Mercer and alderman and worked for the Levant and East India Companies in the Middle and Far East. When he died in 1666 he left most of his estate to Jane who in turn bequeathed the sum of £1,500 for the building of some almshouses.

This sum proved to be inadequate for the purpose and was placed with the Mercers' Company where, after 20 years of accumulating interest it was finally enough to fund Lady Jane's almshouses. In 1690 the company chose the site opposite Stepney Parish Church where the building stands today in its rebuilt form and is still known as Mercers' Cottages although it was taken over by the GLC in 1976 for housing and new ones were built for the Mercers' Company in a modern style in a nearby housing development in Aylward Street.

In the rest of the East End mention should be made of the West Ham United Non-Ecclesiastical Charities buildings in Gift Lane which are currently being renovated, Meggs and Goodwin's almshouses in Upton Lane, West Ham and the Legg-Whittuck Charity for Aged Servants buildings in Forest Lane (also known as the Forest Gate Retreat) built in 1858.

Of those that used to exist, Gibson's almshouses were built in the Ratcliff area in the mid-1530s by Nicholas Gibson together with a school and Esther Hawe's almshouses (1686) used to stand in Bow Lane, Poplar.

To the north Islington was the site of many almshouses, particularly those founded by individuals. Thus Stow's Survey of London records that, in Golding Lane:

Richard Gallard Esq., Citizen and painter-stainer of London, founded thirteen almeshouses for so many poor people placed in them rent free. He gave to the poor of the same almeshouses 2d. the piece weekly and a load of charcoales among them yearly for ever.

Dame Alice Owen's almshouses have now gone although the name Owen appears on two streets near where they were originally built at the top of Rosebery Avenue. John Heath's almshouses for the Company of Clothworkers (1640) and those of Mrs Jane Davis (1794) (both in Queens Head Lane) as well as others in Cumberland Row have also gone although the Bookbinders' almshouses (1843) which used to stand in the Balls Pond Road were rebuilt in 1927 in Bawtry Road, N.20 in a modern style.

However, Islington still contains the Metropolitan Benefit Societies Asylum on the north side of the Balls Pond Road. It was founded by John Christopher Bowles in 1829 although the first stone was laid on 17 August 1836 by the Right Honourable William Taylor Copeland M.P., Lord Mayor of London. The

The upper floor of Stepney's Mercers' Cottages.

date was chosen, according to the inscription on the stone, because it was the birthday of the then Duchess of Kent 'the illustrious patroness of the institution'. It occupies three sides of a large quadrangle set back from the main road, the west wing being named after Mary Ann Mackenzie who left £9,000 to the charity on her death in 1861.

It encloses beautiful gardens where on summer Sundays the perfume of its many roses mingles with the sound of gospel singing coming from a pentecostal church choir using its meeting hall which was rebuilt in 1931. Further north, Sanchez's and Pound's almshouses together with Nicholas Reynardson's (1737) were the earliest in Tottenham and Sir William Staines were relocated from the City to Beaufoy Road where they still stand around a small courtyard beside Tottenham cemetery. But it was the latter half of the 19th century that saw the greatest period of almshouse building in Tottenham including the Asylum for Aged Fishmongers and Poulterers (about 1850) and Printers' almshouses (1856). But two almshouses built in this period that still survive to this day provide excellent examples of the extraordinarily varied types of almshouses that were built in London.

The huge Drapers' almshouses in Bruce Grove were built in 1870 to replace the company's old ones in other parts of London which had been demolished. The almshouses consist of three distinct benefactions which came together over the years under the umbrella of the Drapers' Company. Jolles trust was named after Sir John Jolles who was a master of the Drapers' Company and involved in the plantation of Ireland. He died in 1621 and, after his death the Drapers' Company took over the almshouses he had built in Almshouse Close, Bow. Pemel's trust was founded by John Pemel who bequeathed £1,200 to the Drapers' Company to build almshouses for him after his death in 1681. They were eventually built on a site at Stonebridge in Stepney and opened in 1698. The last charity was that of John Edmanson

Sir William Staines' almshouses tucked away near Tottenham Cemetery to where they were removed from their old site at Jacob's Well Barbican.

The massive Drapers' almshouses occupy a vast site at Bruce Grove in Tottenham.

whose almshouses for old sailmakers were also located in Almshouse Close, Bow near to the Jolles building whose residents were able to use the Edmanson's chapel.

The Bruce Grove site was purchased in 1868 after the North London Railway had come to an agreement with the Drapers' Company for the purchase of Almshouse Close which it needed to widen its track. The Drapers had fought hard in the House of Lords against the railway's plans arguing that the interests of the poor should not be overridden by the narrow interests of a profit making company like the railway. The bill did go through but the railway was forced to buy the whole of the close (which it had not wanted to do), provide temporary accommodation for those residents of the close displaced by their plans and pay all the legal costs of the eventual move to the new site at Bruce Grove. The new Drapers' almshouses stand on the corner of Bruce Grove and Lordship Lane and were built by Herbert Williams. They occupy three sides of a vast enclosure and contain 59 residences (both single and double) and are mostly occupied by local people although back in the 1890s the majority of them had been inhabited by people moved from the old sailmakers' almshouses of John Edmanson. By contrast, the tiny Forster's Cottages in nearby Philip Lane beguile by their sheer charm. The smallest surviving almshouses in London, providing shelter for four widows or spinsters in cosy self-contained apartments, they are now administered by the Quakers. But originally they were built in 1860 and endowed by Josiah and Robert Forster in 1862. The Forster family had moved to Tottenham in 1752 from Birmingham. They became a prominent family in the area and were particularly involved in education, William Edward Forster being the member of Gladstone's Cabinet responsible for the 1870 Elementary Education Act and whose statue can be seen in the Victoria Embankment Gardens by the Thames.

Mrs May Mortimer stands outside Forster's Cottages on a bright summers day in North London.

The former Joel Emanuel almshouses in Egerton Road, Stamford Hill.

Doctor Thomas Wood's almshouses by Clapton Pond founded in 1665 and restored in 1930.

A partial view of Monger House, Hackney.

The Weavers' almshouses in Wanstead.

May Mortimer is proud to be the oldest resident of the cottages both in terms of age and length of stay having lived there since 1963. With their colourful gardens the cottages delight the eye and are one of the gems of London's almshouse heritage. In other parts of north-east London, the former Joel Emanuel almshouses in Egerton Road, Stamford Hill have found a new lease of life as a synagogue and now echo to the sound of young children. Hackney has two sets of almshouses designated as listed buildings of 'special architectural or historic interest'. Bishop Wood's almshouses in Lower Clapton Road behind Clapton Pond were founded in 1665 by Dr Thomas Wood, Bishop of Lichfield and Coventry, who was born in Hackney in 1607. The building was restored in 1930 and its central chimney stack has a sign with the legend 'ALMSHOUSE HELP'. Monger House on the north side of Church Crescent, E9 is also listed. The original almshouses were built in 1670 from a bequest by vestryman Henry Monger. The present building, which dates from 1847, is of two storeys and has gothic touches. The plaque on the façade has faded with time and is now illegible. The almshouses stand in a relatively little known part of Hackney particularly well endowed with buildings of great character from the days when it used to be quite a wealthy area.

As railways began to link London with the surrounding area, two major almshouse projects were undertaken in the 1850s in rural Essex parishes on the fringes of north-east London.

In October 1857 the Worshipful Company of Weavers bought a three-acre site in Wanstead for new almshouses to replace the Company's previous ones at Old Street Road and Porters Field. Joseph Jenning's noble design was opened in July 1859 and a newer block added at the rear when the buildings were reopened in July 1976 by Her Royal Highness Princess Alice, Countess of Athlone. They now give shelter to 41 local people.

T. E. Knightleys' design for the London Master Bakers' Benevolent Institution in Leyton's Lea Bridge Road has also been preserved although it is now used as council housing. It is one of the grand almshouses of north-east London. It is a large three-sided building occupying a large courtyard bordered by the busy Lea Bridge Road to the south, and the Barking to Gospel Oak railway embankment to the west with the ruins of the old Queens Road British Railways goods depot a little way to the north. It has plaques recording the coming of electric light to the 'villas' in 1924 and the installation of gas in 1939 on the wall of the central building. When the foundation stone for this building with its gables, bay windows, towers reminiscent of Iberian church spires and lamp standards set around its large courtyard was laid on 5 August 1857 the area was still a small village with a few villas for wealthy merchants from London. Seen from the top of a nearby block of flats today, the neat streets of terraced houses that were built in the following years as the area was absorbed into London cover Leyton and Walthamstow and stretch to the horizon. But around St. Mary's Church, Walthamstow the atmosphere and architecture of the old Walthamstow Village have been wonderfully preserved including two of the capital's most charming almshouses.

To walk from the busy bus and rail terminal of Walthamstow Central along St. Mary Road to Walthamstow Village is to journey back in time at almost every step. The first turning on the left is Stainforth Road, a residential street so reminiscent of the 1920s that you expect a tram to come trundling along it. At the end of St. Mary Road is a narrow passage called Church Path lined on the left with pretty cottages – some now used as workshops. You then enter Walthamstow Village. It was here that on 6 April 1673 Richard Penn and on 4 March 1681 Lady Penn were buried. They were the brother and mother of William Penn – the founder of Pennsylvania. And today the remnants

Dusk over north-east London silhouettes the skyline of the Bakers' almshouses.

18

of the village's history can be seen in a fascinating collection of architecture. On the right, a 15th century half-timbered house rests lopsidedly on more modern brick restoration work and the excellent Vestry House Local History Museum is to be found in what used to be the parish workhouse. On the left are the six delightful almshouses of Mrs Mary Squires. Founded in 1795 to give shelter to six widows of local tradesmen, all tenants had to be members of the Church of England, over 50 years old and of good moral character and, if accepted, there were many rules governing behaviour. In return for obedience to these, the widows would be housed rent free and receive £12 per annum, coals after Christmas and a loaf each Sunday. Although the regulations sounded rather daunting, the records show Mrs Squires as a widow very much concerned with the well-being of the local poor. She died in 1796 and the almshouses stand today in their peaceful location beside St. Mary's Church virtually unaltered externally since their opening.

About 50 yards further on and to the left walking through the churchyard you then come to the oldest surviving almshouses in London. In 1527 the great benefactor Sir George Monoux founded the first school in the area and almshouses for thirteen poor people on the northern side of the church. Originally both housed in the same building, the school was removed from the second storey to a new location in the 1880s expanding the capacity of the almshouses. The almshouses have been restored and rebuilt several times during their lifetime, the last occasion in 1955 when the western wing was rebuilt to replace the old one which was destroyed in an air raid in 1940. Despite this the building looks very similar to etchings of it in previous centuries. The almshouses stand in their secluded position surrounded by trees and large grounds containing a graveyard. In one corner of the graveyard the final resting place of a couple killed in an air raid during the Second World War lies close to that of a rifleman killed in the First. The almshouses are administered by

Mary Squire's almshouses founded in 1795 in Walthamstow Village.

the Walthamstow Almshouses and General Charities who are also responsible for Jane Sabina Collard's almshouses (1881) in Maynard Road, E17 which were rebuilt in 1974 in the style of a modern housing development.

Further to the south, there have been almshouses adjoining Leyton Parish Church since 1656 when John Smith's almshouses were opened. The present building dates from later having been officially opened on 9 February 1886. They were built by D. Sayer and designed by Richard Creed in a tudor style and the use of flint and stone in their construction, the low single storey design and the position of the almshouses nestling amid the greenery of the churchyard in Church Road combine to give a strikingly vivid impression of what it must have been like to live in a humble and isolated rural almshouse.

As can be seen, the relatively little known districts of north-east London provide some of the most beautiful and interesting examples of London's almshouses. Often hidden away, they have survived to enhance the architectural and historic heritage of these areas. Although not as concentrated as those in north-east London, the other parts of the city also contain many almshouses of great interest and beauty that have survived the years together with memories of many others which used to exist.

Sir George Monoux's almshouses and graveyard under stormy skies, Walthamstow Village.

Sir George Monoux's almshouses.

Winter in Walthamstow. A blanket of snow covers the graveyard around Monoux's almshouses.

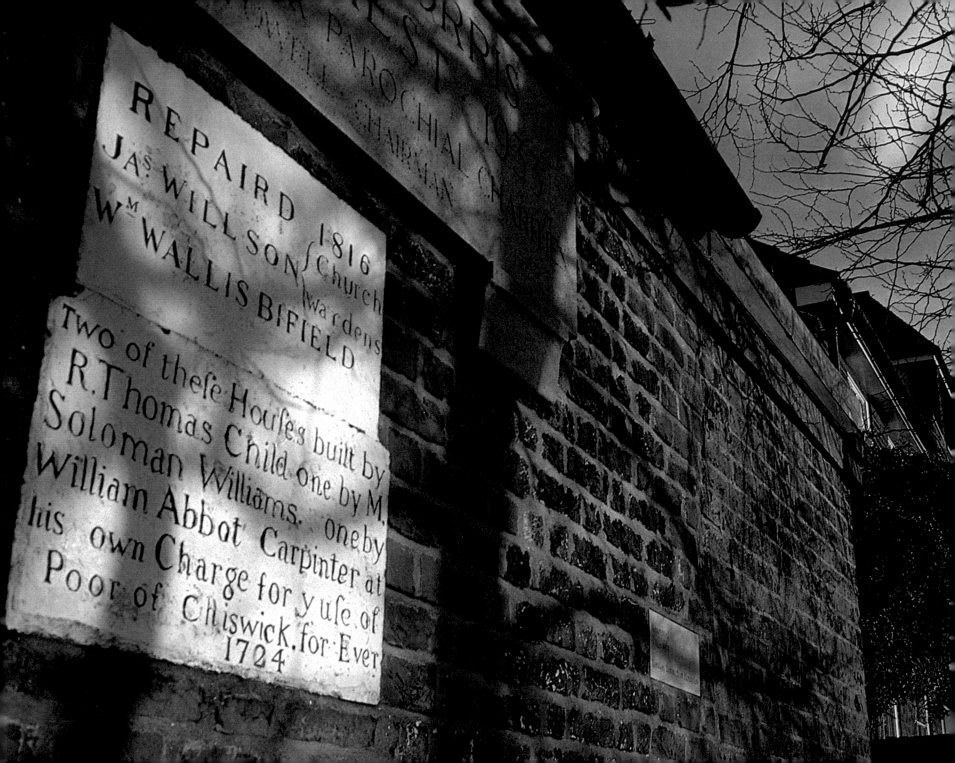

REPAIRD 1816
JAᵒ WILLSON Church
Wᴹ WALLIS BIFIELD wardens

Two of these Houses built by
Rᵗ Thomas Child one by Mᵗ
Soloman Williams one by
William Abbot Carpinter at
his own Charge for y use of
Poor of Chiswick for Ever
1724

2
THE CITY, CENTRAL LONDON, HIGHGATE AND THE WEST

The figure of Richard (Dick) Whittington has passed into legend as the poor lad who came to London and became Lord Mayor. As with many legends the facts are somewhat different as he came from a fairly wealthy family. However, one fact that those children and adults who have watched Dick Whittington pantomimes might not have realised is that he played an important part in the history of London's almshouses.

In his will dated 5 September 1421 he bequeathed all his tenements in the parish of St. Andrew near Castle Barnard and in the parishes of St. Michael Bassishaw and St. Botolph without Bishopsgate to his executors John Coventry, John Carpenter and William Grove. Under the will his executors founded a college of priests and an almshouse called Whittington's almshouse which was completed by December 1424. Both buildings were situated by the church of St. Michael Paternoster (which Whittington had founded) just south of Cannon Street at the southern end of College Hill, the almshouses being behind the site of what is now the office of the Finnish bank Kansallis–Osake–Pankki and is called Whittington House.

The almshouses accommodated one tutor and twelve residents and the ordinances for governing the behaviour of the inhabitants were strict and religious. At daily prayers the almspeople had to pray for the souls of Richard and his wife Alice, Richard's parents Sir William and Lady Joan Whittington, Alice's parents Sir Hugh and Dame Matilda Fitzwarren and Richard II. They had to recite paternosters when they got up,

went to bed and during their spare time. The almspeople were not allowed to leave the almshouses at any time without the permission of the tutor. These regulations were relaxed in 1552 and 1560 when new ordinances were introduced. Most inhabitants were freemen of the City of London from City Livery Companies and they took their meals with the priests from the college.

The significance of Whittington's almshouses was that, athough not the first to be founded in London, they established the idea of wealthy men and City Livery Companies founding almshouses for the poor of London. They were the forerunners of the many almshouses built by City Companies in north-east London and other areas. In 1822 the Mercers' Company decided to rebuild Whittington's almshouses. A site was chosen close to Whittington's stone in Highgate which marked the spot where Dick was supposed to have heard the sound of Bow Bells although the stone that was there in 1822 was the third, having been placed there the previous year by the parish. The building on Highgate Hill was designed in the gothic style by George Smith who, 34 years later, was to be responsible for the rebuilding of Lady Jane Mico's almshouses in Stepney. In between he also designed St. Paul's School (1823–24), the Corn Exchange (1827–28) with Arthur Bowyer Clayton, St. Albans Courthouse and Town Hall (1829–33) and London Bridge Railway Station (1841–44) with Henry Roberts which was demolished in 1969.

The Highgate Hill almshouses had 30 residences (13 for the people from College Hill and a further 17 for people nominated by individual members of the Court of Assistants) and a chapel. By 1962 the Ministry of Transport had made it known that it wanted to widen Highgate Hill and compulsorily purchase part of the Whittington buildings. The Mercers' Company made several attempts to get permission to rebuild them in the area but eventually decided to rebuild them at Felbridge near East Grinstead in 1965 removing from Highgate the organ from the chapel and Joseph Carew's statue of Richard Whittington. Of the other almshouses that once stood in the City of London none remains. Guy Shuldham's will of 7 November 1446 endowed thirteen Vintners' almshouses which originally stood by the Vintners Hall in Thames Street. They were burnt down in the Great Fire of London in 1666 and were re-erected at the western end of the Mile End Road. Burnt down again during the Second World War they were rebuilt at Nutley in Sussex. John Hasilwood's will of 16 January 1544 instructed the Leather-sellers' Company to purchase the site of the old St. Helen's monastery and build a hall and seven almshouses. They stood in St. Helen's Place off Bishopsgate until the late 1700s when they were pulled down. Two houses in nearby Clarkes Court were appropriated to accommodate the four almsmen and three almswomen.

The Merchant Taylors' Company built almshouses at Tower Hill in 1593. In a unique scheme, the fourteen almswomen placed in them were provided for by gentlemen nominated by the court. He could provide for her upkeep direct or pay a sum of money to the Company to do it for him. In 1637 the Company decided to add twelve more. They were rebuilt in 1767 but in 1825 the Company decided to move its almshouses south of the river to the leafy district of Lee where they were built in 1826.

Robert Rogers' almshouses (1601) in Hart Street, Cripplegate and Gresham's almshouses in City Mews were also moved south of the river to the site of the London almshouses in Ferndale Road, Brixton built by the Corporation of the City of London (see Chapter 3). Sir William Staines' almshouses in Jacobs Well, Barbican were moved to Beaufoy Road, Tottenham.

There used to be Salters almshouses in Bow Lane, founded by Thomas Beaumond in 1454 and Monkwell Street, founded by Sir Ambrose Nicholas in 1578. The Dyers Company's first almshouses were founded in 1545 by Sir Robert Tyrwhilt in White Cock Alley, Thames Street and were followed by those of Henry West in Holborn and William Lee in St. John's Street, Spitalfields (1721). In 1771 the Tyrwhilt and West almspeople were moved to new almshouses in City Road. In 1841, the Spitalfields almshouses were closed and new accommodation found in the Balls Pond Road where all the almspeople were brought together in 1851 before being moved out of London to Crawley in the 1930s.

Lord Sudbury's charity founded almshouses in Hart Street which were turned into a workhouse in 1738. George Palyn's almshouses were built in 1612/13 in St. Luke's Old Street for six poor people. Destroyed in the Great Fire they were rebuilt in Pesthouse Row but by 1849 they had become delapidated and were removed to a site in Peckham given to the Girdlers' Company (who were trustees of the Charity) by Mr Thomas Watkins.

Mrs Susan Amyas died in April 1651. In a deed gift of the previous year she directed that eight almshouses should be built after her death. Building commenced in 1655 in George Yard, Old Street. They were rebuilt from 1749–54 at a cost of £200 but the almshouses became the victims of the squalor around them. In 1807 Mr Wigginton, Beadle of Old Street Liberty, found some dead cats in the cellar of almshouse number 3. They had been flayed. In 1820 a police officer was paid a sum of money for recovering lead which had been stolen from the roof of the almshouses. They had become unsafe and were rebuilt again from 19 August 1871 to 8 May 1872. In 1891 a committee was set up following the death of a resident in a paraffin lamp explosion. However, the committee was unable to improve the lighting of the houses and the use of the lamps continued until the almshouses were demolished.

Possibly the most beautiful almshouses ever built in the City were Milbourne's almshouses (1535). On 24 November 1534 Sir John Milbourne (a former Lord Mayor of London) bought a site next to the Church of the Convent of Crossed Friars and built thirteen almshouses. Made of brick and timber and partly faced with stone they were located in what is now Coopers' Row just north of the Tower of London, although an illustrated plaque on the wall just outside Tower Hill Underground station notes that from 1252–1750 it was called Woodroffe Lane after an English woodland flower and that Sheriff David Woodroffe lived there in 1554. In a deed dated 5 March 1535 Sir John transferred the almshouses to William Dolphin and his heirs. Sir John died on 5 April 1536. He directed that, after his death, his thirteen 'bedesmen' as he called them, should daily visit his tomb in the Church of the Crossed Friars and say the psalm *De Profundis*, a paternoster and a creed. The almshouses were enclosed by a gateway above which was a sculpture of the assumption of the Virgin, two armorial shields (of Sir John and his wife Joan) and below them two other shields of the Drapers and the Merchants of the Staple. Beneath was a Latin inscription which read:

Ad laudem Dei et gloriore Virginis Marie hoc opus erexit dominus Johannes Milbourne miles et alderman' hujus civitatis AD 1535.

This was later replaced by an English version. In the 1860s the residents of the almshouses (now sixteen in number) were relocated by the Drapers and the old almshouses were demolished and replaced by warehouses.

Further afield, in what is now the legal part of London, there used to be almshouses on the site now occupied by the Royal Courts of Justice in the Strand. The St. Clement Danes Holborn Estate Charity was founded in 1552 by the churchwardens of St. Clement Danes church. Some time after 1700 they acquired almshouses behind Clement's Inn Hall. Accounts of this part of London during the next decades show it to have been somewhat less than salubrious with squalid tenements and unsafe streets. The almshouses were replaced in 1849 by new ones at Garratt Lane in Tooting (see Chapter 3). Dyers Buildings off Holborn stand on the site of the previously mentioned eight Dyers almshouses founded by Henry West in the 1500s.

Gray's Inn Road was originally a horse track called Gray's Inn Lane leading to Highgate and used by traders from the Midlands on their way to and from markets in the City. In his will of 10 May 1651 Alexander Stafford of High Holborn transferred his ten newly built almshouses to his trustees. The almshouses gave shelter to four men and six women from the Upper Liberty parish of St. Andrew, Holborn and stood on a site called Liquorpond Field where the Royal Free Hospital is now situated. John Wright's benefaction of 24 May 1659 provided coats for the men and gowns for the women of Stafford's almshouses at Michaelmas every two years but this was later discontinued. There were extensive repairs costing £90 in 1817 but the almshouses were eventually demolished.

Macklin Street is a tiny street in Holborn lined with old tenement buildings and workshops. Opposite a three-storey tenement called Powis Buildings, on the north side of the street between the many printing and design studios that are now situated in the street, at 17a is the only remaining almshouse in the centre of London. A small blue painted wooden doorway in a blank brick wall bears the name St. Giles-in-the-Fields' almshouses. Behind the wall and its grey painted railings can be seen the chimney stacks and top floor of these two-storey almshouses.

Behind the door is a sight unknown to the many people who pass by the unremarkable brick wall. A minute courtyard perhaps 15 feet wide and 50 feet long. In the middle a tree stands. Small in any other setting, here its branches and leaves seem to fill the courtyard. Ivy climbs up the eastern wall and in summer the flowers and bushes around this enclave burst into colour. The almshouses occupy the west and north sides of the yard. Two benches enable the residents to enjoy this cramped but cosy nook in the centre of the busy streets of central London. Various plaques and a large clock are attached to the inside of the Macklin Street wall. The almshouses of St. Giles-in-the-Fields had originally been built in 1656 right in the middle of the high street at the intersection of Shaftesbury Avenue and St. Giles High Street facing Monmouth Street on ground given by the Earl of Southampton. There were five brick almshouses for widows containing two rooms each. The congestion they caused coupled with their decayed state prompted an appeal to the attorney general Chief Justice Kenyon in August 1782 by the vestry to demolish them and build new ones.

This resulted in a new site being purchased in 1783 in Lewknors Lane (Macklin Street) between Swordbearers Alley and the Coal-Yard and the erection of the new and larger almshouses of St. Giles-in-the-Fields and St. George Blooms-bury (although the heir to the Earl of Southampton's estates, the Duke of Bedford promptly built on the site of the old ones in the middle of the high street until he was assured compensation for giving up the site to allow better traffic flow). Later, in the words of local chronicler Walter Blott writing in 1892:

In 1885, the Alms-house Committee, wisely or otherwise re-erected these cheerless homes for the aged poor in this foul cul-de-sac at a cost of £2,723 4s. 0d.

Although conditions have improved since then and the alms-houses are well looked after it is not difficult to imagine what this cramped area of narrow streets between Kingsway and Shaftesbury Avenue would have been like in the late 1700s and during the 19th century. The grey soulless slums, noise and poverty that the almspeople would have had to endure would have been very different from the atmosphere those lucky enough to live in the quieter almshouses such as those at Walthamstow Village would have enjoyed.

The St. Martins-in-the Fields' almshouses had stood (before 1681) close to Charing Cross. In 1683 they were relocated on a plot of land called Kemps Field (Charing Cross Rd) and housed 60 women from the parish of St. Martins-in-the Fields. By the early 1800s the parish needed new burial grounds and they were established in St. Pancras. It was further decided to rebuild the almshouses in 1817/18 next to the burial grounds at Bayham Street near the intersection with Pratt Street in Camden Town where they still stand although there have been many changes recently (the beautiful almshouse church at the back has been converted to housing).

The burial ground contained the tomb of Charles Dibdin (died 25 July 1814) who was a local resident and popular and prolific song writer of his day (e.g. Poor Jack). Of his songs it was written:

Though they amount to upwards of twelve hundred, it may truly be said, that while a great proportion of them are in praise of love and festivity, not one passage can be found in the whole number of a loose and licentious tendency. On the contrary, they

St. Giles-in-the-Fields almshouses, Holborn; the Macklin Street entrance.

Partial view of the St. Giles-in-the-Fields almshouses in their cramped courtyard in central London.

are calculated to support the interests of virtue, and to exercise the best affections of the heart, as well as to enforce the duties of loyalty and patriotism.

HISTORY OF ST. PANCRAS
SAMUEL PALMER 1870

The memorial to Dibdin in the centre of the grounds put up by the Kentish Town Musical Society still stands although the other tomb stones are now scattered around the grounds. To visit them now is a sad experience. The human tragedy of this ill-fated part of London is on show – a powerful reminder of the realities of poverty and hopelessness which prompted the founding of the city's almshouses and which still exist today.

The Camden Town and Kentish Town almshouses founded by Mrs Esther Greenwood of Cumberland Terrace, Regent's Park now stand in Rousden Street off the Camden Road and not far away in Southampton Road off Haverstock Hill by St. Dominic's Priory the St. Pancras almshouses still survive as sheltered accommodation. They are amongst the most pleasing buildings in this part of London. Founded in 1850 by Donald Fraser M.D. and rebuilt in 1859 they are constructed of sturdy brick and the three sides enclose a delightful expanse of lawn framed by trees and beautifully kept. The gardens in summer are breathtaking in the variety and colour of the flowers and there are seats placed around the lawn together with old fashioned lamp standards.

Up at Highgate Village at the southern end of Southwood Lane are the twelve single storey almshouses of Wollaston and Pauncefort. Sir John Wollaston (a goldsmith) founded six almshouses in 1656 and left their administration to the governors of Highgate School (around the corner). They were rebuilt in their present form in 1722 by Sir Edward Pauncefort – one of the governors and treasurers of Highgate School. Although not

visually attractive in themselves, they are of great interest for their antiquity, humble design and position in this extremely beautiful part of London's northern heights close to the heart of Highgate Village.

In the City of Westminster, south of Hyde Park, all the old almshouses which once stood have disappeared and been replaced by a single institution – the United Westminster almshouses in Rochester Row (1881). It is the result of a decision of 11 July 1879 of the Charity Commissioners to amalgamate three of the old Westminster almshouses plus the charity of Mrs Hannah Chadwick. The present almshouses (30 in number) were built at No. 42 Rochester Row on the site of one of the original almshouses – those of Mr Emery Hill whose name appears on a nearby street.

His twelve single-storey almshouses with a schoolroom and chapel were built in 1708 when the area was known at Tothill Fields. Six of the houses were for couples and six for widows. The couples received 16s. per month and the widows 14s. together with coals and gowns. In addition under Mr Hill's will of 10 April 1677 a stock of sea coals was kept in store nearby to help the poor of Westminster during bad winters.

In 1656 the Reverend James Palmer founded twelve almshouses, a chapel and a school house off Little Chapel Street (Caxton Street) near Brewers Green in Tothill Fields. The area became known as Palmer's Village and there is still a Palmer Street in the area today. The almshouses were rebuilt in 1816/17 but eventually incorporated into the United Westminster Almshouses.

The third component was Nicholas Butler's two almshouses built in 1675/76 at a cost of £232 1s. 0d. close to Palmer's almshouses in York-House Yard, Little Chapel Street.

The present U.W.A. buildings in Rochester Row were designed by R. R. Arntz and modernised in 1962. Apart from the 30 residences (6 for couples and 24 for single people) there

The St. Pancras almshouses framed by trees.

Wollaston and Pauncefort's almshouses in Highgate Village.

is accommodation for a matron, caretaker and a house for the warden. On the outside walls either side of the almshouses are plaques recording the original almshouses and busts of Emery Hill and the Reverend Palmer.

These charities have been lucky in that they have been able to continue their good works although the original buildings are no longer with us. George Whicher's six almshouses for men (1680) in Little Chapel Street and Judith Kifford's two almshouses for women (1705) opposite Palmer's almshouses in Brewers Green were relocated in Lambeth and north of Hyde Park the Christian Union almshouses still survive in Crawford Place off the Edgware Road. But the other almshouses which used to grace the southern parts of Westminster have not been so fortunate. All have now disappeared under the flood of wealthy residences and offices which have swamped the area over the last 150 years.

Lady Anne Dacre's almshouses, (The Emanuel Hospital) founded in 1594 and built in James Street in 1600 consisted of single-storey buildings with high chimney stacks, a chapel with a clock tower and crest surrounding three sides of a lawn and occupying one acre. They were taken down at the turn of the century.

King Henry VII's almshouses stood in the Little Almonry and were for thirteen men. The Charity Commission report of 1815–39 recorded that they had been taken down some years before under a scheme for improving Westminster Lady's Alley's almshouses (1741) for four women stood in St. Anne's Lane although they took their name from a previous location off King Street (believed to have been founded by James I for women whose fathers or husbands had been employed in the royal household or in the King's service). They had also existed in St. Stephen's Alley (Cannon Row) but were moved to St. Anne's Lane when demolished to make way for the building of Westminster Bridge as were Woolstaple's almshouses

The central building of the United Westminster almshouses in Rochester Row

(Hospital of St. Stephen) which had stood in a street known as Woolstaple (now Bridge Street). Rebuilt in St. Anne's Lane in 1741 they numbered eight and were also known as the Waterman's almshouses because many of the residents had been watermen of the Thames.

It appears from the Charity Commission report that by the 1800s the almspeople made a good living by letting out their almshouses. In the 1830s three of the almshouses were being let to William Hummerston who repaired and sublet them himself. The house belonging to Mrs De Perrin was being let for £3 5s. per year to Mr Thomas Andrews, a publican, who also sublet it. A house which had been let out by a pensioner called Sloat who died in 1814 to an Elizabeth Chambers was still inhabited by her rent free. And another one had been let out by William Loft Senior to a bricklayer called Joseph Stock who promptly declined to pay any rent, refused to leave and took over an adjoining almshouse to store lumber – the roof of this one subsequently collapsing. The Charity Commissioners' report on Woolstaple's almshouses ends with the following words:

> The present state of this charity, is evidently such as to require the attention of the proper authorities.

The other almshouses which used to stand in Westminster were those of Cornelius Van Danne – his name being anglicised to Vandon. He had been born at Breda in Brabant but came to England and was a yeoman of the guard and usher to King Henry VIII, Edward VI, Queen Mary and Queen Elizabeth. He founded two sets of almshouses in Westminster. One set was in Petty France on land bought by Cornelius from the Dean and Chapter of Westminster. Permission to begin building the almshouses was obtained on 30 June 1572. The almspeople were nominated by the Dean of Westminster, the minister or curate of the parish and the two churchwardens. The original six almshouses built by Vandon were augmented in 1677 by three

more built by the parish from a legacy of £100 from Emery Hill (+ £10 from local builder Emery Argus). Two people lived in each almshouse giving them a total capacity of eighteen. He also founded another set near St. Ermin's Hill at the west end of Tothill Street which numbered eight. The Petty France almshouses (also known as the Red Lion almshouses) had originally numbered eight as well but two had quickly fallen into disrepair by the time of the Emery Hill legacy. Indeed by the time of the report of the Charity Commissioners in the mid-1800s all of Vandon's almshouses were in bad condition with the exception of those built under the Emery Hill legacy. Both sets of almshouses were inhabited at this stage by old women who were mostly former housekeepers.

A visit to the sites of the old Westminster almshouses today reveals few traces of them. St. Anne's Lane is now a narrow passage of faceless modern flats and offices. Palmer Street is much the same at its southern end. At the western end of Petty France is Vandon Street and the Vandon House Hotel together with a passage and a building near the Passport Office named after him. His other almshouses are believed to have stood on the site of the St. Ermin's Hotel in Caxton Street. James Street is now Buckingham Gate and the St. James' Court building stands on the site of Lady Dacre's almshouses. Woolstaple is now the Bridge Street which runs alongside Big Ben to Westminster Bridge, the building of which was responsible for the removal of the area's almshouses. To the west, the old almshouse buildings which used to stand in the fashionable districts of Kensington and Chelsea have now disappeared with the exception of St. Joseph's almshouses on the south side of Cadogan Street which are now being renovated to be let to the elderly.

Methwold's almshouses were built around 1650 by William Methwold. They were for six poor women and built around a large courtyard facing onto Cromwell Lane. This is now the vacant site in Harrington Road, Kensington in front of St. Augustine's Church beside the empty and derelict Imperial Hotel. By the 1860s the Metropolitan District Railway wanted the site for its line. By an act of 1867 the railway company paid £3,750 to the Kensington Vestry to acquire the site. No almshouses were to be built in their place. Instead the money would be used to provide a stipend for the poor women of Kensington. As it turned out the railway did not need the land after all. But the almshouses were emptied by October 1873, demolished shortly afterwards and the land sold to the builder William Douglas.

Under swingeing powers for the removal of buildings occupied by the poor taken by the parish authorities, the Gravel Pits' almshouses were pulled down shortly after 1820. They had stood in the High Street, Notting Hill Gate. The rents from the houses built in their place were applied to the parish's poor rate. Hammersmith had three major almshouses. Dr Ile's almshouses (the Brook Green almshouses) stood in Brook Green and were founded in 1629 (later amalgamated into the Waste Land Charity). The almshouses of the Butchers' Charitable Institution were founded in 1828 for 'affording relief to decayed or distressed master butchers, master pork-butchers, cattle and meat commission salesmen, their widows and orphans'. They were begun in 1840 at Walham Green and consisted of a double row of houses in Vanston Place Road (later moved to Middlesex).

The third were William Smith's almshouses for Protestants founded in 1865 and built in 1868 behind Lower Mall in Hammersmith in what is now Macbeth Street. Hammersmith now has a United Charities organisation with premises in Sycamore Gardens off the Goldhawk Road in which are combined Iles and Waste Lands charities and Smiths almshouses and at Rylett Road where the benefaction of Dr. John Betts

was built in 1964. A fourth charity, that of the Aged Poor Society has pensioners' homes in Brook Green.

In neighbouring Fulham in Fulham Palace Road stand the modern Wasteland almshouses. Sometimes called the new almshouses to distinguish them from Sir William Powell's (see below) they had originally been built in two phases in 1833 when seven almshouses for couples were opened and 1837 when seven more were built for single people. They had stood on the north-west corner of Estcourt Road facing Dawes Road and contained a small library. But they are the most recent of the Fulham almshouses. John Lappy's almshouses and others in Bear Street (Burlington Road) existed in Fulham in the 1600s but it was in 1680 that Sir William Powell, a local landowner and Member of Parliament for Hereford, founded almshouses in Burlington Road. They were rebuilt in 1793 by Nathaniel Chasemore although the Reverend R. G. Baker noted that old materials were used which resulted in them having to be extensively and expensively repaired.

But it was in 1869 that the new Sir William Powell almshouses were built on their present site by Fulham Parish Church on land bought from the Ecclesiastical Commissioners in Churchgate. Built by W. Wigmore they were designed by J. P. Sedden and the foundation stone was laid on 15 May 1869 by the Reverend Baker.

Of all the almshouses that were ever built in London these must rank as some of the most beautiful and unusual both for their design and their position. They occupy two sides of a rectangular piece of ground enclosed behind a high hedge next to the church yard. Sedden's gothic design for these two-storey almshouses is breathtaking for the sheer beauty of the design and the intricate stone work all along the façade and on the tower by the gate which includes an inscription recording the charity together with sculptures of Biblical women (Miriam, Anna, Deborah, Dorcas, Ruth and St. Mary) and the faces of faith, charity and hope. There is an expanse of lawn and the lovely gardens burst into a riot of colour every spring and summer. Each almsperson looks after a section of the garden. It is a building which would grace a university or religious institution. To be discovered in West London as a home for the poor is all the more astonishing. Because to look at this little known building, one of the hidden gems of London's architecture, is not only to gain pleasure from the sight of a beautiful building. It is an experience because it is so totally at odds with the way we are taught to imagine how the poor and in particular the elderly are supposed to live. This sturdy and magnificent building has tremendous dignity as well as beauty. It is the imagination, care and concern that went into it which are as stunning as the building itself. After seeing a building like this, it is impossible to look at the high rise blocks of today with anything other than deep regret.

Of the rest of west and north-west London, the work of charitable shelter for the poor is carried on in modern almshouses in St. John's Wood Terrace, at Wilmot Close in Finchley on the site of the old Finchley almshouses and at the large sites on either side of Hammer Lane in Mill Hill where the Linen and Woollen Drapers' Cottage Homes are. Just around the corner along The Ridgeway can also be found Thomas Nicolls' six almshouses (1696).

In West London, Goldsmith's almshouses (the sister buildings to those that used to stand in East London) are in East Churchfield Road, Acton near the railway level crossing and are now rented out on normal commercial terms although members of the Worshipful Company of Goldsmiths are given preference. In Ealing and Chiswick there are several modern charities but Princess Amelia's almshouses which were built on the Uxbridge Road in Ealing between the Common and the Broadway have gone as have Chiswick's Sutton Lane almshouses founded by Chaloner Chute in 1659.

Hidden beauty. Sir William Powell's almshouses were founded in Fulham in 1680 and rebuilt on their present site in Churchgate in 1869. An unnoticed gem of London's architecture.

However, one small trace can be found of an ancient Chiswick almshouse. On the pretty Thames side walk at Strand-on-the-Green inlaid in the wall of the B. Hopkin Morris Homes of Rest can be seen a small white tablet. It records the founding of the original almshouses on this spot in 1724 – two by Thomas Child and one each by Solomon Williams and William Abbott.

For many people the districts of the City and central London are London. Their streets, squares, monuments and buildings are well known to visitors and Londoners alike. Symbols of wealth, power and imperial history. The fact that they once contained and still contain many almshouses for the care of the poor and elderly is a much less well known aspect of their history.

To discover these buildings is to reveal a little appreciated face of the city.

The tower of Sir William Powell's almshouses seen from the grounds of Fulham parish church.

Biblical statutes in Sir William Powell's almshouses.

3
SOUTH OF
THE RIVER

If the districts of South London have been traditionally regarded as the poor relations of those north of the Thames, it is not surprising that there should have been a need for almshouses to provide shelter for the inhabitants of these poor areas. What perhaps is surprising is that it should have been met with some of the capital's largest and most impressive almshouses in districts not normally known for their architectural merit.

In 1848 work was begun on the new almshouses for the St. Clement Danes Holborn Estate Charity on the corner of Garratt Lane and New Road (now Wimbledon Road) in Tooting to replace their old buildings north of the river. The Building Committee and the architect Mr Hesketh visited all the alms-houses in the vicinity of London in order to get a clear idea of what was needed and to take the best ideas from them and incorporate them into the proposed new almshouses.

The resulting building was opened on 12 July 1849 in a ceremony which took place in the large Devotional Room in the centre of the main building. On advice from the Solicitor of the Attorney General a much larger area of land was procured than was actually necessary for the construction of the 40 residences (some 6 acres in all) so as to provide a vast garden at the front for the health and enjoyment of the inhabitants. The water supply came from an Artesian well which was so plentiful that it was able to support a large fountain in the gardens. Possibly the most ingenious development made by Mr Hesketh was the system of alarms that was installed linking each individual residence to the matron's house. At the head of each bed was a bell-pull. If any of the almspeople needed help, a gentle tug on this would set off an alarm in the matron's house and in addition an indicator consisting of a piece of iron painted white would fall in front of the door of the resident in need of help

Although most of the almspeople would be elderly, as Mr Twinning one of the trustees said in his opening address:

They are not merely for the reception of those who are so far advanced in life, that their enjoyment of a residence here can only be calculated upon for a very limited period; but persons are selected, who, although at, certainly, advanced periods, may yet be expected, under God's blessing, to find this a peaceful and happy refuge for many years to come.

An excellent statement of the aims of all almshouses. And of the almspeople he said:

Above all, we entreat you to be watchful that no strife, nor wrath, nor contention ever find their unhallowed entrance within these peaceful boundaries. 'Be kindly affectioned one to another.' 'Bear ye one another's burdens.'

This vast red brick building survived for many years in its role as an almshouse. On 22 October 1952 Her Majesty Queen

An aerial view of the former St. Clement Danes Holborn Estate Charity almshouses in Garratt Lane, Tooting.

A view of the east wing of the St. Clement Danes Holborn Estate Charity almshouses.

Elizabeth The Queen Mother unveiled a tablet on the façade of the Devotional Room commemorating the 400th anniversary of the foundation of the charity. In 1966/67 the trustees sold the buildings to Wandsworth Council and the almshouses are now used as council housing. The St. Clement Danes Estate Charity built new almshouses in a pleasant modern design on Wells Park Road in Sydenham. In surrounding areas, the old 41 grey brick and stone almshouses of the Fishmongers' Company which used to stand in East Hill, Wandsworth and were known as St. Peter's Hospital were pulled down in the 1920s to make way for L.C.C. flats although the Company's other almshouses at Bray near Maidenhead (founded in 1616) and Harrietsham near Maidstone (founded in 1642) are still in existence.

The Thrale's almshouses for four ladies which used to stand in Streatham High Road and were built in the 1820s were demolished in 1931 much to the sadness of all who knew them. Dovedale Cottages stand in Battersea Park Road.

The Hibbert almshouses founded in 1859 for the elderly of Clapham still stand at the western end of the Wandsworth Road near its junction with Lavender Hill and further on in Putney Bridge Road are the almshouses of Sir Abraham Dawes which were founded by this wealthy man in 1627. They have now been extensively renovated.

Further afield at Knight's Hill in Norwood the almshouses of the Society of Friends of Foreigners in Distress were founded in 1851 but demolished in 1898 to make way for Norwood Technical College.

To the north in Brixton Thomas Bailey's almshouses (Trinity Homes) were erected in 1822 in Acre Lane where they still stand although uninhabited in 1984 but the area does contain an almshouse site of great interest.

In the early 19th century, Parliament was facing a major crisis. When the Great Reform Bill of 1832 was passed there was much rejoicing throughout the land that the country had been spared something far worse. On 23 May Thomas Attwood, one of the major figures in the agitation for the bill, was given a banquet in the Guildhall and presented with the Freedom of the City in gratitude for the fact that, in the words of George Grote the banker and historian speaking at the banquet:

He has taught the people to combine for a great public purpose, without breaking any of the salutary restraints of the law . . .*

In a further act to commemorate the passing of the Bill, the Corporation of the City of London decided to found the City of London Freemans' Houses (or Reform Almshouses) in what is now Ferndale Road, Brixton. Rebuilt in 1884 they became known as the London almshouses and were designed by the architects Davis and Emmanuel. In the early 1880s two other sets of almshouses which had stood in the City were relocated on this large site. Robert Roger's almshouses which had stood in Hart Street, Cripplegate were rebuilt on the east side of the site and Gresham's almshouses, originally in City Mews were also moved there.

This accounts for the difference in design between the two-storey red brick buildings on the west side of the enclosure with their balconies and display of hanging flower pots and the separate blocks on the east side which house the two relocated benefactions. Nearby in Coldharbour Lane used to stand the almshouses of the Company of Parish Clerks for eight widows. A few hundred yards further to the north up Brixton Road are some more almshouses in possibly the strangest and most unexpected position of any in London. The Friendly almshouses were founded in 1802 by the Friendly Female Society and built in 1863. Damaged in 1941, the building was restored in 1947

*Quoted in Butler, J.R.M., *The Passing of the Great Reform Bill* (*Frank Cass* 1914).

Thomas Bailey's almshouses (Trinity Homes) stand in Acre Lane, Brixton.

The London almshouses in Ferndale Road, Brixton were originally founded in 1832 to commemorate the Great Reform Act.

out of funds from the Lord Mayors National Air Raid Distress Fund.

It now stands in a small cul-de-sac surrounded by the vast, sprawling Stockwell Park housing development, a tribute to the durability of London's almshouses. Further to the north off the Camberwell Road between Albany Road and Neate Street stands what used to be known as the Friendly Female Asylum which were the original almshouses built by The Friendly Female Society. The building was erected in 1821 in what was then Gloucester Place (now Chumleigh Street) and a tablet on the building recorded the following:

THE FRIENDLY FEMALE ASYLUM
FOR AGED PERSONS
WHO HAVE SEEN BETTER DAYS
ERECTED AND SUPPORTED
BY VOLUNTARY CONTRIBUTIONS
1821

One of the patrons was Queen Victoria but unfortunately it is now the building that has seen better days. Renamed Chumleigh House it has fallen into disrepair. Its gardens are now overgrown and untidy and the building itself was being used in 1984 as a squat by a group of young people. A sad memorial to the original charity. In Lambeth, the original almshouses built in the Wandsworth Road in 1623 by Sir Noel de Caron (the Dutch Ambassador in England from 1609-1624) were pulled down but new ones for seven widows erected on some of his property in Fentiman's Road beside Vauxhall Park just to the south west of the Oval cricket ground. They still exist today and are known as Noel Caron's Houses. Behind them in Stanley Close is the site for Kifford and Whicher's almshouses which were moved to Lambeth from Westminster in 1855.

Robert Roger's almshouses, Ferndale Road, Brixton.

Just south of Blackfriars Bridge off Southwark Street are the almshouses of Hopton's Charity. They were founded by Mr Charles Hopton in 1730 for inhabitants of the parish of Christ Church, Surrey in what was then called Holland Street. They were completed by 1749 but not opened until 1752. The street subsequently took his name and the almshouses still survive despite the many changes on the South Bank in recent years which have left them surrounded by office blocks and other commercial buildings. Just to the south in Burrell Street, Edward Edwards' almshouses were founded in 1717. They were rebuilt in Clapham Road and on the 31 May 1973 Princess Anne opened a new building called Edward Edwards' House in Nicholson Street just a few yards south of the original Burrell Street Location. In Brandon Street are the modern John Walters almshouses for 26 single people and 15 married couples.

However, it is in Southwark that London's largest almshouse was built and can still be seen to this day. The Licensed Victuallers' Benevolent Institution was founded in Asylum Road in 1827 and the first stone was laid on 29 May of the following year by the Duke of Sussex. The original intention was to built 43 residences but the project expanded into London's largest such institution. The first construction was the central almshouse building which occupies three sides of the main quadrangle and includes an impressive portico supported by ten pillars (eight rounded and two square).

However, this in turn was surrounded by an even larger three-winged almshouse building (in effect an almshouse surrounded by another almshouse) which gives the site a total capacity of some 176 residences. The outer ring of almshouses contains a southern wing which is called the Albert Wing after the royal consort Prince Albert who laid the foundation stone for the block that was to bear his name on 23 June 1858 some nine years after he had done the same for the Ladies' Wing. Designed by Charles Arding and built by J. Mortimer the Albert Wing

Down and out. Chumleigh House used to be the Friendly Female Asylum but is now overgrown and used as a squat.

Carons Homes in Fentiman Road, Lambeth were originally founded by the Dutch ambassador Sir Noël de Caron in 1623 in the Wandsworth Road.

A wing of Hopton's almshouses in Southwark.

was completed in August 1862 with the erection of thirteen almshouses. The royal connection continued and two years later HRH The Prince of Wales unveiled a statue to Prince Albert in the almshouse chapel behind the central façade. It was subsequently moved to the new victuallers' homes in Denham. A large ornamental gateway was added in 1927 to commemorate the centenary of the founding of the building. Although the building is now used as council housing, the gateway still stands and the tablets recording the royal wing can still be seen inlaid in the wall of the outer southern almshouse. The building continues to provide a refuge of peace and quiet in an area of London where this is a rather rare commodity. A few years after the establishment of the Licensed Victuallers' almshouses, the Metropolitan Beer and Wine Trades Society's Asylum was founded. The first stone was laid on 9 June 1852 by Lord Monteagle and the building still stands today on Nunhead Green.

South-east London contains the city's most distinguished almshouses. The history of Morden College, Blackheath is long and illustrious and has been well documented already by others. As this is intended as a general survey of the development of almshouses in London it is not my intention to repeat it in detail here. However briefly stated it is as follows. Sir John Morden Bt. (born 1623) was a member of the Turkey Company trading in the Middle East. While serving on the committee responsible for supervising the construction of what is now the Royal Naval College at Greenwich he met Sir Christopher Wren and it was to him that Sir John turned when he decided to found an almshouse (or college in the non-educational sense of a place where people live together). The college was for poor merchants who had fallen on hard times and building was begun in 1695 with the first residents being admitted five years later. Sir John administered the institution himself until his death in 1708 whereupon it was taken over by the Turkey

A partial view of the central building of the former Licensed Victuallers' Benevolent Institution founded in Southwark in 1827.

The Metropolitan Beer and Wine Trades Asylum, Nunhead Green.

Morden College in Blackheath. The autumn sun illuminates one of London's most distinguished almshouses.

The clocktower of Morden College.

Company until 1826 and the East India from 1827 to 1884. From then to the present day it has been administered by the Court of Aldermen of The City of London which appoints the trustees of the college who are all former Lord Mayors of London. With its magnificent design, croquet lawn, putting green, club house and location amid 11 acres in one of outer London's wealthiest and most exclusive areas it is a building to be admired like a stately home or palace. The aristocrat of London's almshouses a world away from the small humble almshouses of Macklin Street or Leyton.

There are two other large almshouse institutions in southeast London. St. Saviours United College in Hamilton Road, Gipsy Hill and the Merchant Taylors' almshouses in large and beautiful grounds on the corner of Brandram Road and Lee High Road. The garden is full of trees, flowers and shrubs and at the front of the grounds on Lee High Road is the one surviving building from the original almshouses of Christopher Boone – the chapel. Boone, a wool merchant originally from Taunton built four almshouses on this site in 1683. In addition a chapel was built and also a house for a school mistress whose job it was to teach English and religion to twelve poor children of the parish. The residents of the almshouses were able to take in washing and grow provisions in little plots. Religion played a major part in the life of Boone's almshouses. One of the qualifications for admission was that you should be able to recite by heart the Lord's Prayer, the Apostle's Creed and the Ten Commandments. If you could not achieve this within two months of entry you were liable to be expelled. Regular attendance to services in the chapel was also expected. In 1813 the chapel was made the temporary parish church for the area while a new one was being built. The pride that this bestowed was perhaps slightly dented by the unfortunate incident in that year when, during morning prayers one Wednesday, a horse and cart unable to slow down to negotiate the junction outside

Residents enjoy the grounds of Morden College.

St. Saviours United College gateway, Gipsy Hill.

The Merchant Taylor's almshouses, Lee.

The Brandram Road entrance.

The Merchant Taylor's almshouses grounds.

the chapel, crashed through the main door of the building upon a startled but mercifully unharmed congregation.

The chapel (believed to be the work of Sir Christopher Wren) still stands today on the north side of Lee High Road on the slight bend in the road just past the bus stop. Boone's almshouses were demolished in 1877 and relocated on a site on the other side of the road a few hundred yards further to the east on the corner of Lampmead Road. These buildings together with the new chapel that was built also still survive although Boone's almshouses were rebuilt in 1964 by the Merchant Taylors' Company (who have been the trustees of Boone's charity since his death in 1686) in a pleasant modern style in Belmont Park just a short way from the Merchant Taylors' own almshouses.

Ironically, the two south London almshouses most closely associated with the maritime world are to be found some five miles from the Thames in suburban Penge. 'Most prominent building in Penge' is perhaps not a major architectural accolade but, if such an award existed, it would undoubtedly go to the enormous almshouses of the Free Watermen and Lightermen which dominate the High Road. Built by George Porter in 1840–41, this vast grey building stands at the corner of Penge Lane and the High Road beside St. John The Evangelist's Church. In the centre of the quadrangle is a memorial to the founding father of the asylum John Dudin Brown. The buildings occupy three sides of the site and, although Porter's design with its magnificent gate-tower, turrets, trestled stone walkways across the gardens and eccentric stone creatures on pedestals at the entrances to the gardens may not be to everyone's taste, there is no mistaking the care and concern of the original foundation or of the restoration of 1920 which, as a shield on the gate-keeper's house makes clear, was undertaken as a memorial to all the freemen and apprentices of the Worshipful Company of Watermen and Lightermen of the Thames who died during the Great War.

However, just around the corner on the west side of St. John Road is the hidden jewel of south London's almshouses. Almost invisible behind a screen of trees and bushes stands a three-sided red brick and stone building. There is little now to identify it but the building used to be the King William IV Naval Asylum. Founded in 1847 by Queen Adelaide to the memory of King William, the two-storey building is now used as council housing, the previous naval residents having been moved some years ago. Designed by Philip Hardwick, the beautiful red brick houses have great dignity and a cedar tree stands in the middle of the luxuriant grounds – the enclosure now being known as King William IV Gardens.

It is meant as no disrespect to the larger institutions, but the greatest pleasure is often to be found in discovering the small, unpretentious, out-of-the-way almshouses that London has to offer. They are often passed by, unnoticed by many locals and unknown by outsiders, but they provide some of the most beautiful buildings in the city. If west London can boast Sir William Powell's almshouses and the north-east Forster's Cottages and Mary Squire's almshouses, south London is no less well endowed.

This is not to ignore the fact that life in these more humble dwellings could be difficult. For example, the almshouses of the Canterbury born vicar Abraham Colfe in Lewisham High Street were ordered to be closed in 1905 by the sanitary authorities. Founded in 1664 seven years after Colfe's death, the building was designed by Peter Mills and run by the Leathersellers' Company. When threatened with closure these five single-storey flint and brick almshouses were saved by a public subscription matched by a donation from the Company until demolished some years ago.

The enormous Free Watermen and Lightermens' Asylum dominates Penge High Street.

A view of the Free Watermen and Lightermens' Asylum.

The King William IV Naval Asylum in St. John Road, Penge is now used as council housing.

William Hatcliffe was Chief Officer of King James' stables. In his will of 15 May 1620, after bequeathing £30 to his sister Anne Duck to buy mourning clothes, he directed that his land in East Greenwich, Lee and Lewisham should be used for the relief of the poor of those areas. In 1857 the trustees of Hatcliffe's charity decided to build almshouses in Lewisham and Greenwich. One set was built in Rushey Green on the site of what is now Lewisham Town Hall. They were rebuilt in 1925 in Bromley Road but destroyed in an air raid during the war.

The names of Colfe and Hatcliffe now appear together on a modern residential building on the east side of Lewisham High Street called Colfe's and Hatcliffe's Glebe.

The Hatcliffe's almshouses that now stand in Tuskar Street, Greenwich were built in 1938 out of money bequeathed to the charity by four Greenwich ladies: Adelaide Mary Smith, Henrietta Martyr Smith, Mary Jane Smith and Ellen Mortimer Smith of Croom Hill. The building still stands but is a sad and neglected monument. Largely decayed and boarded up, only three of the almshouses are still inhabited although there are plans for its renovation.

Lewisham High Street still has many buildings of character at its southern end near Rushey Green. On the corner of the High Street and Feldam Road are the six yellow brick almshouses for aged females built in 1840 by John Thackeray of The Priory, Lewisham who died on 13 May 1851.

Apart from the Bethel Asylum for twelve aged women founded by William Peacock in 1838 in Havil Street, Peckham can boast one of the most attractively situated almshouses in London. Cuthbert Beeston was a Master of the Girdlers' Company and founded seven almshouses near the old London Bridge in 1582. The Company sold the site in the 1820s to the builders of the new London Bridge and the money was used to fund the building of Beeston's Gift almshouses in Peckham. The site, on the corner of Consort Road and Scylla Road now also

William Hatcliffe's almshouses in Tuskar Street, East Greenwich.

The Bethel Asylum in Havil Street, Peckham.

houses George Palyn's almshouses (originally in the City before being moved first to Choumert Road in 1851 on land given by Thomas Watkins and then to the Consort Road site) and those of Richard Andrews. The beautiful grounds are enclosed by a screen of trees and the shady, flower filled gardens combine perfectly with the cool white almshouses. It is an indication of the range of different styles of almshouses that have been built over the centuries in London that even an area of such major architectural and historic distinction as Greenwich which can claim some of the most impressive buildings in the capital still has space for three of the most charming almshouses in London. In the shadow of the Royal Naval College on a bend in the Thames near Lovell's Wharf is Trinity Hospital. Founded by Henry Howard, Earl of Northampton in 1613 its accommodation was to be divided between twelve locals and eight men from Howard's birthplace in Shottesham, Norfolk (or Rising or Bungay if enough worthy people could not be found in Shottesham). The first residents were admitted on 24 February 1617 but the statutes of Trinity Hospital made it very clear the sort of people they didn't want. The resident:

shall be a man that is decayed, and is become poor by casual means, and not through his own dissolute life, and one that hath always lived in honest name. No common beggar, drunkard, whore-hunter, haunter of taverns nor ale houses nor unclean person infected with any foul disease, nor any that is blind, or so impotent as he is not able, at the time of his admission to come to prayers daily ... nor any idiot, nor any other that is not able to say, without book, the Lord's Prayer, the Creed and the Ten Commandments.

The chapel of the almshouses was consecrated on 4 February 1616 by the Bishop of Rochester and the statue of Henry

The clocktower of the ancient Trinity Hospital in Greenwich.

A view of Trinity Hospital from the riverside walk.

Trinity Hospital. The Old Woolwich Road entrance.

Howard which had stood in the chapel of Dover Castle was later relocated in the south east corner of the almshouse chapel.

Although dwarfed today by a power station they still excite interest from those visitors to Greenwich who walk to the end of the riverside promenade to the small promontory in front of the almshouses. Underneath the clock tower which still strikes the hour, a passage leads to a small courtyard where sunlight catches the sparkling water from a fountain giving an almost Moorish touch. Behind the building are large grounds which stretch to the Old Woolwich Road wall.

Opposite Greenwich station in Greenwich High Road is Queen Elizabeth College founded by William Lambard in 1576 – the same year that saw the publication of his celebrated county history *Perambulations of Kent* to add to his legal works. The services at the almshouses' own chapel were compulsory but this did not stop the almshouses being struck by bubonic plague in 1636 in an attack which led to the sealing off and virtual closure of the building. The delightful almshouses on the site today date from 1819 and occupy three sides of a leafy quadrangle with additional accommodation behind. They house 40 people. The tiny chapel in the centre of the middle building with its portico, clock and bell tower is still used and the almswomen attend in their Sunday best each week.

A few hundred yards to the west along the High Road used to stand the Jubilee almshouses. In 1809 George III celebrated 50 years on the throne and the Greenwich Parish Officers organised an appeal which totalled £1,153. 13s. Most of this was used to provide meat, bread, potatoes, a quart of porter and a peck of coals to the poor of the parish but with the £447. 6s. left over it was decided to build four almshouses for widows. Other contributions included proceeds from the sale of John Kimbell's famous account of Greenwich charities published in 1816 and by 1866 there were 20 almshouses on the site. In 1883 it was decided to rebuild them facing the High Road to celebrate the jubilee of Queen Victoria due in four years time. The foundation stone was laid in 1888 by Princess Beatrice and Prince Henry of Battenburg and the building was officially opened on 2 March of the following year by the Earl of Dartmouth. The total number of residences was 31. They were demolished in 1974 and new flats built retaining the name 'Jubilee'. The third set of surviving historic almshouses in Greenwich are those of John Penn and Widow Smith. John Penn was an engineer with a works in Blackheath Road and eight almshouses were founded in 1884 after his death by his widow Ellen. A further two were added when Widow Mary Ann Smith's charity was included in the Penn benefaction. Widow Smith's almshouses had been founded in 1866 in Trafalgar Road near the Royal Naval College. The almshouses stand in Greenwich South Street and are a striking red brick affair with white dressing around the windows and parapets like icing on an elaborate cake. An impressive memorial to the man they were named after and to their architect whose name appears on the central plaque. It is that of George Smith – one of the last of the prolific architect's works to be built.

London possesses a magnificent but largely unappreciated architectural and historic heritage in its almshouses. To visit them is to see the city in a totally different light to the usual one. The city of commerce and wealth and state pageantry becomes a city of hidden architectural jewels, colourful gardens and dignified homes for the poor. That so many have survived the years is a tribute to the founders of the past and the trustees and residents since. As London develops and the pressure to pull down old buildings and put up new offices and flats continues it is to be hoped that these historic buildings will be protected and will survive to be enjoyed and admired for many years to come as symbols of architecture for people rather than profit or prestige.

EPILOGUE

The concept of almsgiving, of charitable help for the poor, can take many forms. Probably the most well known example being the distribution of the Royal Maundy money each Easter by the Queen although the much less well-known provision of so-called 'grace and favour apartments' in some royal properties such as Hampton Court and some of the London palaces is also a shining example of this. Nor is it an exclusively Christian concept. Other cultures have their own versions such as the traditional Muslim festival of Aid el Kebir in North Africa in which portions of meat are distributed to the poor. But nowhere have the ideals of almsgiving produced such a heritage as in the almshouses for the shelter of the poor which can be found all over Britain and in particular the extraordinary and unique collection of historic buildings that continue to quietly and unobtrusively grace the streets of London.

From the great ministries of state of Westminster to the homes of the rich and powerful in Belgravia London is a city steeped in history. The history we are taught at school is that of the great events and figures. History is not history unless it has a politician or general, war or great cause in it. But there is a vast layer of history which is rarely appreciated. The lives of ordinary people, the culture and flavour of their everyday lives are rich and perhaps were we to learn more of our own and other cultures, we would get a more balanced and realistic view of history.

Whether or not the term 'community architecture' was known to Sir Richard Whittington or Dame Alice Owen, they practised it all those centuries ago in a form which helped the most urgent and basic need of the poor of London's often squalid streets – a home of their own and freedom from despair. A paternalistic form of help? By its very nature it had to be. A product of the deep rooted class divisions which existed then and still exist today and which in some ways have divided us as surely as Catholic and Protestant in Ulster or Christian and Muslim in Lebanon. But in a city where the lives of rich and poor would rarely meet the divide was at least partially bridged by this form of almsgiving and by the tradition of compassion and concern for the less fortunate which is one part of the English heritage. Had the wealthy individuals behind some of the city's almshouses merely wanted prestige or a place in history, a statue or some equally useless monument would probably have sufficed. That they chose to use their money in the construction of these buildings demonstrated an awareness of ordinary people's lives and concern for the poor as did the involvement of the city livery companies and their extensive and invaluable contribution to the almshouses of London. Other London institutions took on the role of almshouses as part of their functions – most notably the Royal Hospital in Chelsea founded during the reign of Charles II as a hospital for elderly and invalided soldiers and Charterhouse in EC1, off Aldersgate Street, originally founded in 1371 as a Carthusian monastery but later to become one of the great English educational institutions and including a 'hospital' founded by Thomas Sutton.

Faced with an individual case of poverty in everyday life most will shy away. But here is a uniquely useful and practical way to face up to a problem and help. And not just a stop gap solution but homes of dignity and pride. The contrast between the solution of the almshouse founders and designers and the high-rise blocks of modern times could not be more stark. The almshouse builders for the most part recognised the need for buildings for people on a human scale – where people could mix and talk and a community spirit could flourish. But this was something that the politicians, planners and architects responsible for tower blocks allowed themselves to forget (or never appreciated in the first place) in their rush to build a brave new world of highrise blocks in the 1950s and 1960s. By no means was it always for bad reasons. The old and decaying housing stock in bomb damaged areas like Leyton Road in north-east London needed replacing. But it was replaced by badly built highrise slums which were themselves blown up by the local council in the early 1980s. An expensive way to learn a lesson which most ordinary residents would have regarded as plain commonsense anyway. The legacy of planning for statistics rather than for people continues to affect us today. Faced with rising crime and violent street disorders in the inner cities more and more police forces employ architectural advisers to help with understanding the problems of inner city architecture. Ironically, the lessons that the almshouse builders learnt centuries ago are unconsciously being relearnt today in new attempts to plan for a better quality of life in such concepts as 'community architecture'. And in Bow in London's East End can be seen one of the most hopeful signs of this new awareness. At the foot of three tower blocks in Rainhill Way the only surviving wing of Edmanson's almshouses in what used to be Almshouse Close has recently been brilliantly renovated in an award winning development for a housing association. In an area which has seen much modern development (including some thought provoking and original designs for modern low-rise blocks and small arcades of shops) it is the old almshouse building which had fallen into decay and could so easily have been swept away that is one of the symbols of the new concern and interest in public housing and shows in a tangible way that these little appreciated buildings for so long ignored could hold important lessons for a more enlightened public housing policy responsive to human needs.

At a time of great social pressure and division when so called meritocracy and 'Victorian Values' are espoused by some, it is to be hoped that the story of the almshouses of London may give pause for thought on the whole question of attitudes to the poor and ways of helping them.

HOW TO GET THERE

 UNDERGROUND STATION IN AREA

 NEAREST BRITISH RAIL STATION

🚌 A SELECTION OF L.R.T. BUS ROUTES THAT LINK CENTRAL LONDON
WITH DISTRICTS CONTAINING HISTORIC ALMSHOUSES

NORTH-EAST LONDON

	Underground	British Rail	Bus
Drapers Almshouses, Bruce Grove, Tottenham	Seven Sisters	Bruce Grove	171[a]
Edmansons Almshouses, Rainhill Way, Bow	Bow Road		25
Emanuel Almshouses, Egerton Road, Stamford Hill		Stamford Hill	76
Forsters Cottages, Philip Lane, Tottenham	Seven Sisters	Seven Sisters	171[a]
Ironmongers Almshouses (Geffrye Museum), Kingsland Road, Dalston	Old Street	Old Street	22, 48
London Master Bakers Benevolent Institution, Lea Bridge Road, Leyton	Walthamstow Central	Leyton Midland Road	38, 48, 55
Mercers Cottages, Stepney High Street	Stepney Green	Stepney East	10, 25
Metropolitan Benefit Societies Asylum, Balls Pond Road, Islington	Highbury & Islington	Dalston Kingsland	30, 38
Monger House, Church Crescent, Hackney	Bethnal Green	Cambridge Heath	6
Monoux Almshouses, Walthamstow Village	Walthamstow Central	Walthamstow Central	
Norton Folgate Almshouses, Puma Court, Spitalfields	Liverpool Street	Liverpool Street	6, 8
Smiths Almshouses, Church Road, Leyton	Leyton	Leyton Midland Road	
Squires Almshouses, Walthamstow Village	Walthamstow Central	Walthamstow Central	
Staines Almshouses, Beaufoy Road, Tottenham	Seven Sisters	White Hart Lane	171[a]
Trinity House Almshouses (Trinity Green), Mile End Road	Whitechapel		10, 25
Weavers Almshouses, Holly Bush Hill, Wanstead	Leytonstone		10
Woods Almshouses, Lower Clapton Road		Hackney Central or Clapton	38, 48, 55

THE CITY, CENTRAL LONDON, HIGHGATE & THE WEST

	⊖	⇌	🚌
Christian Union Almshouses, Crawford Place, Edgware Road	Edgware Road		6, 8, 15, 16
Goldsmiths Almshouses, East Churchfield Road, Acton		Acton Central	
Powell's Almshouses, Churchgate, Fulham	Putney Bridge		11, 14, 27, 30
St. Giles-in-the-Fields Almshouses, Macklin Street, Holborn	Holborn		22, 38, 55
St. Martins in the Fields Almshouses, Bayham Street Camden Town	Camden Town	Camden Road	24, 27, 29, 31, 53, 74
St. Pancras Almshouses, Southampton Road, Haverstock Hill	Chalk Farm	Primrose Hill	24
Strand-on-the-Green Almshouses Plaque (B. Hopkin Morris Homes of Rest), Strand-on-the-Green, Chiswick	Gunnersbury	Kew Bridge	27
United Westminster Almshouses, Rochester Row, Westminster	Victoria	Victoria	All Services to Victoria Bus Station
Wollaston & Paunceforts Almshouses, Southwood Lane, Highgate Village	Highgate		

SOUTH OF THE RIVER

	⊖	⇌	🚌
Beestons Gift Almshouses, Consort Road, Peckham		Peckham Rye	12, 36, 36ᵃ, 63, 171
Bethel Asylum, Havil Street, Peckham		Peckham Rye	as above
Boones Chapel, Lee High Road		Lewisham	21
Carons Homes, Fentiman Road, Lambeth	Vauxhall	Vauxhall	2, 28, 36, 36ᵃ, 36ᵇ, 77
Dawes Cottages, Putney Bridge Street, Putney	Putney Bridge		30
Dulwich College, Gallery Road, Dulwich		West Dulwich	2, 3, 63, 196
Free Watermen & Lightermen's Asylum, Penge High St		Penge East	12
Friendly Female Asylum (Chumleigh House), Chumleigh St, Walworth			12, 45, 68

	⊖ (Underground)	⚡ (British Rail)	🚌 (Bus)
Greshams Almshouses (London & Rogers Almshouses), Ferndale Road, Brixton	Brixton	Brixton	2, 2b, 3, 45, 159
Hatcliffes Almshouses, Tuskar Street, Greenwich		Maze Hill	1, 188 to Greenwich
Hibbert Almshouses, Wandsworth Road, Clapham		Clapham Junction	77, 77a
Hoptons Almshouses, Hopton Street, Southwark	Blackfriars	Blackfriars	45, 76
King William IV Naval Asylum, St. John Road, Penge		Penge East	12
Licensed Victuallers Benevolent Institution, Asylum Road, Southwark	New Cross Gate	Queens Road (Peckham)	36, 36a, 53
Merchant Taylors Almshouses, Brandram Road, Lee High Road		Lewisham	21
Metropolitan Beer & Wine Trades Asylum, Nunhead Green		Nunhead	12
Morden College, Blackheath		Blackheath	53
Penn's Almshouses, Greenwich South Street		Greenwich	1, 188
Queen Elizabeth College, Greenwich High Road		Greenwich	1, 188
St. Clement Danes Holborn Estate Charity Almshouses (Ex), Garratt Road, Tooting	Tooting Broadway	Haydons Road/Earlsfield	44, 77
St. Saviours United College, Hamilton Road, West Norwood		Gipsy Hill	3
Thackerays Almshouses, Lewisham High Street		Lewisham	21, 36, 36a, 185
Trinity Homes, Acre Lane, Brixton	Brixton	Brixton	2, 2b, 3, 45, 159
Trinity Hospital, Lovells Wharf, Greenwich		Greenwich	1, 188

This list shows Underground and/or British Rail Stations which are in the area of the historic almshouses mentioned in the book.

None of these stations is immediately adjacent to the buildings and a good A-Z guide is essential. Please note that some of the British Rail stations mentioned (particularly north of the Thames) are on local lines which do not originate at the main line termini in central London. Please consult B.R. information offices for details of these services. North of the Thames the tube should be easier and more frequent in theory. The bus routes mentioned are only a brief selection, of those that link the areas concerned with central London. Please consult the L.R.T. London Wide bus map for full details.

At all times respect the privacy of the almspeople.

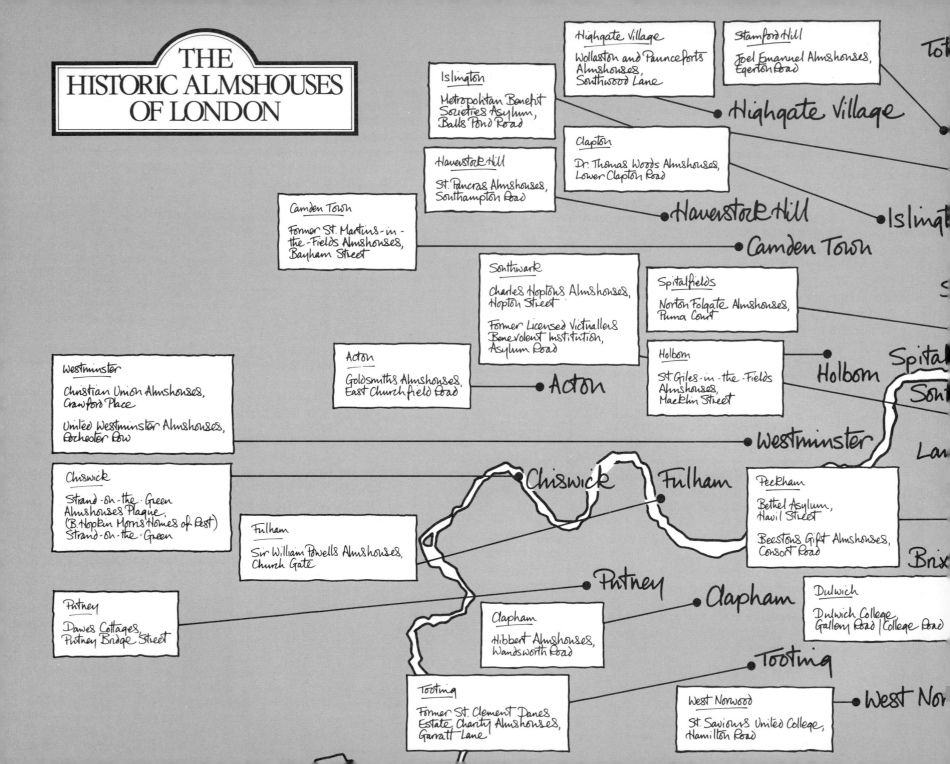

THE HISTORIC ALMSHOUSES OF LONDON

Highgate Village
Wollaston and Paunceforts Almshouses, Southwood Lane

Stamford Hill
Joel Emanuel Almshouses, Egerton Road

Islington
Metropolitan Benefit Societies Asylum, Balls Pond Road

Clapton
Dr. Thomas Woods Almshouses, Lower Clapton Road

Haverstock Hill
St. Pancras Almshouses, Southampton Road

Camden Town
Former St. Martins-in-the-Fields Almshouses, Bayham Street

Southwark
Charles Hoptons Almshouses, Hopton Street

Former Licensed Victuallers Benevolent Institution, Asylum Road

Spitalfields
Norton Folgate Almshouses, Puma Court

Acton
Goldsmiths Almshouses, East Churchfield Road

Holborn
St. Giles-in-the-Fields Almshouses, Macklin Street

Westminster
Christian Union Almshouses, Crawford Place

United Westminster Almshouses, Rochester Row

Chiswick
Strand-on-the-Green Almshouses Plaque, (B. Hopkin Morris' Homes of Rest) Strand-on-the-Green

Fulham
Sir William Powells Almshouses, Church Gate

Peckham
Bethel Asylum, Havil Street

Beestons Gift Almshouses, Consort Road

Putney
Dawes Cottages, Putney Bridge Street

Clapham
Hibbert Almshouses, Wandsworth Road

Dulwich
Dulwich College, Gallery Road / College Road

Tooting
Former St. Clement Danes Estate Charity Almshouses, Garratt Lane

West Norwood
St. Saviours United College, Hamilton Road

Highgate Village

Haverstock Hill

Islingt

Camden Town

Holborn

Spital

Sou

Westminster

La

Chiswick   Fulham

Brix

Putney   Clapham

Tooting

West Nor

Tot

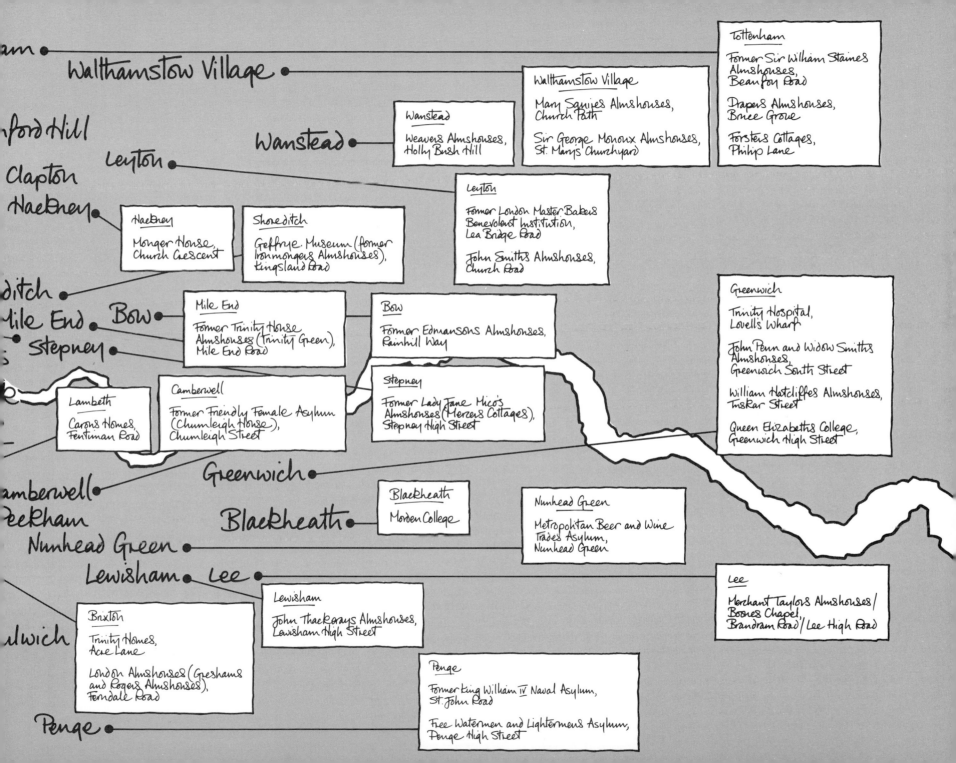

Walthamstow Village

Tottenham

Former Sir William Staines Almshouses, Beaufoy Road

Drapers Almshouses, Bruce Grove

Forsters Cottages, Philip Lane

Walthamstow Village

Mary Squires Almshouses, Church Path

Sir George Monoux Almshouses, St. Mary's Churchyard

Wanstead

Weavers Almshouses, Holly Bush Hill

Leyton

Former London Master Bakers Benevolent Institution, Lea Bridge Road

John Smiths Almshouses, Church Road

Hackney

Monger House, Church Crescent

Shoreditch

Geffrye Museum (former Ironmongers Almshouses), Kingsland Road

Mile End

Former Trinity House Almshouses (Trinity Green), Mile End Road

Bow

Former Edmansons Almshouses, Rainhill Way

Greenwich

Trinity Hospital, Lovells Wharf

John Penn and Widow Smiths Almshouses, Greenwich South Street

William Hatcliffes Almshouses, Tuskar Street

Queen Elizabeths College, Greenwich High Street

Stepney

Former Lady Jane Mico's Almshouses (Mercers Cottages), Stepney High Street

Camberwell

Former Friendly Female Asylum (Chumleigh House), Chumleigh Street

Lambeth

Carons Homes, Fentiman Road

Blackheath

Morden College

Nunhead Green

Metropolitan Beer and Wine Trades Asylum, Nunhead Green

Lewisham

John Thackerays Almshouses, Lewisham High Street

Lee

Merchant Taylors Almshouses/ Boones Chapel, Brandram Road/Lee High Road

Brixton

Trinity Homes, Acre Lane

London Almshouses (Greshams and Rogers Almshouses), Ferndale Road

Penge

Former King William IV Naval Asylum, St. John Road

Free Watermen and Lightermens Asylum, Penge High Street

SOURCES AND ACKNOWLEDGMENTS

Books

Ashbee, C. R. *The Trinity Hospital in Mile End: an object lesson in national history*, Guild School of Handicraft, 1896.

Beaver, A. *Memorials of Old Chelsea*, Elliot Stock, 1892.

Besant, Walter, *East London*, Chatto and Windus, 1901.

Blanch, William Harnett, *Ye Parish of Camberwell*, E. W. Allen, 1877.

Blott, Walter, *A Chronicle of Blemundsbury*, Walter Blott, 1892.

Butler, J. R. M., *The Passing of the Great Reform Bill*, F. Cass, 1914.

Charity Commission Reports, 8/10/12/14/17 & 20 relating to the City of London, 1823–29.

Charity Commission Report, Vol. 22, London & Westminster, 1815–39.

Clarke, Ebenezer, *The History of Walthamstow*, Joseph Shillinglaw, 1861.

Colvin, *Biographical Dictionary of British Architects*, 1600–1840, J. Murray, 1978.

Duncan, Leland, *History of the Borough of Lewisham*, North, 1908.

Faulkner, Thomas, *A History of Hammersmith 1839*, London, 1965.

Feret, C. J., *Fulham Old and New*, The Leadenhall Press, 1900.

Fisk, F., *History of Tottenham*, Frederic Fisk, 1913.

Gordon, Edward and Deason, A. F. L., *The Book of Bloomsbury*, Edward Gordon, 1950.

Hatcliffe, William, *The Will of William Hatcliffe*, Henry Richardson, 1857.

Imray, Jean, *The Charity of Richard Whittington*, Athlone, 1967.

Jackson, Edith, *Annals of Ealing*, Phillimore & Co, 1898.

Kennedy, J., *History of the Parish of Leyton, Essex*, Phelps & Co, 1894.

Kimball, John, *An Account of the Legacies, Gifts, Rents, Fees, etc. Appertaining to the Church and Poor of the Parish of St. Alphege Greenwich in the County of Kent*, G. Allen, 1816.

Major, Henry, *Jubilee Alms-Houses Greenwich – a Short Statement of Their Foundation, History and Re-building*, E. G. Berryman & Sons, 1889.

Milbourne, Thomas, *The Milbourne Almshouses and a Brief Account of the Founder and His Charity*, publisher unknown, 1867.

Mitton, G. E. and Geikie, J. C., *The Fascination of London: Hammersmith, Fulham and Putney*, Black, 1903.

Moreland, John, *An Account of the Almshouses of Mrs Susan Amyas*, R. E. Taylor & Son, 1905.

Palmer, Samuel, *History of St. Pancras*, Samuel Palmer, 1870.

Parton, John, *Some Account of the Hospital and Parish of St. Giles-in-the-Fields Middlesex*, L. Hansard, 1822.

Stows, *Survey of London*, J. Wolfe, 1598, as well as many others.

Tanswell, John, *The History and Antiquities of Lambeth*, Picton, 1858.

Reference and Local History Libraries/Archives/Museums

I would like to express my grateful thanks to the local history and reference librarians, archivists and other staff of the following for their help in the preparation of this work:

Reference and local history libraries

Battersea	Guildhall	Lewisham	Tottenham
Chelsea	Holborn	Leyton	Victoria (Westminster)
Fulham	Kensington	Shoreditch	
Greenwich	Lambeth	Stoke Newington	

Archives, museums and others

Bruce Castle Museum	Morden College
Drapers' Company	Royal Netherlands Embassy, London
Dyers' Company	St. Clement Danes Holborn Estate Charity
Fishmongers' Company	St. Saviours United College
Friendly almshouses	Salters Company
Girdlers' Company	United Westminster Almshouses
Hammersmith United Charities	Vestry House Museum Walthamstow
London Borough of Hackney	Vintners Company
Mercers' Company	Worshipful Company of Goldsmiths
Merchant Taylors' Company	Worshipful Company of Weavers

My special thanks go to Brian Hill and Doug and John Pethick, Roy Heywood, John Sinkins and all without whose help this would not have been possible.

Residents

Last but not least, I would like to thank the many residents of London's almshouses who helped in the production of this book by providing information or allowing me to photograph their homes.

Almshouses are peoples' homes and private property. The purpose of this book is to foster interest in and appreciation of these unique buildings: Most can be admired from the public highway. But for closer inspection permission should be obtained from the trustees or residents.

INDEX